Janet N. Gold

Local Fare
poems from midcoast Maine

Janet N. Gold

Local Fare
poems from midcoast Maine

ISBN: 978-0-692-84093-1

Author photo – Stephen Gold
Cover design and layout – Richard Reitz Smith
Cover illustration, "Ornamental Jewelweed" by Linda Funk

janetngold@gmail.com • janetngold.com

For my Grove Street neighbors

and for Stephen

Contents

I. The Old Norway Maple

II. The Islands of Summer

III. Each in Its Season

The Old Norway Maple

I wonder
if the old Norway maple
knows I write poems
about it?

Trash Tree

Trash tree he called it,
that gaunt Norway maple.

Invasive, too.

Sending its offspring
with defiant determination
into our beds of
carefully pruned
specimens and cultivars.

An old-timer:
stubborn
strong-willed
endowed with a persistent core
of life and fight.

And here I am
petulantly contemplating
its asymmetry
as if this breathing trunk were flawed
because it is dying
too soon for my taste!

Turning Wheels and Pastel Helmets

Rider the first glides by
cautious fingers
on the handbrakes
eyes looking ahead
to the flat stretch
after the downhill
swoosh
nine years old
but feeling ten
sometimes seven
her heart
zipped inside her pink parka
rushes toward
the red brick school.

Rider the second in blue and purple
follows her lead
the backpack of a new day
bundled with curious compositions
and hesitant hopes.

Ride, girlfriends, ride
your green and yellow bikes
past your neighbors' windows
as they drink their coffee
read the morning paper
and scold the world
for disappointing them.

That small glide of turning wheels
and pastel helmets
makes us pause
look up at the sky
see three crows
watching
from the second branch
of the gaunt Norway maple.

Busy Elsewhere

Crow the large is first to land
on the west limb
of the gaunt Norway maple.

Black as coal another
and curious crow alights
on the metal fence.

I wait by the window.

But they are busy
elsewhere this morning,
have no messages for me
from the moonless night
or the cemetery on the hill.

The Yellow Bus

A black bird flies
to an inner branch
of the old Norway maple.

Another lands higher up.

Father and son
step onto their porch.

An arc of sunlight
opens the room.

The purple tulips
in the glass vase
open their faces
and turn oh so slowly
toward the window.

A hug and a kiss
and the blue-jacketed boy
boards the yellow bus.

The Sky Turns Pink

Three small birds
just flew out
of the waning crescent moon
dipped like a shiny soup ladle
into the pale gray broth
of the morning sky.

How did they get there?

How did they fit
in the skinny belly
of that weary grandmother moon?

The Norway maple reached out
and offered its brittle branches
but the three small birds,
unweary,
had other things to do
than perch and watch
the sky turn pink.

Day of Light and Laundry

On this day
of light and laundry
a lift of the heart
and then
an unmatched sock
brings you close to tears.

A sunpatch slants
among fallen brown leaves
and you draw in your breath
with the surprise
of remembering.

The rake scrapes
singles into piles
over and over
and then
its claws uncover
an unwary blossom.

What were you thinking,
arm or rake or flower?

All the unknowing
pushes you
into an unlit corner
where you linger
in late morning musings
as the bedsheets flap on the line
in the neighbor's backyard.

That Unrehearsed Melody

A crow on a branch
of that old Norway maple
and then another
a third alights
and off they fly
to the backyard trees.

They are free to go
and return
as is the lone gull
and the loon who passes
on his daily flight
from lake to bay
and the cardinal couple
always in tandem
and the robins in late winter
nipping at the wrinkled burgundy crab apples.

They range over our plots
and lots and garden fences
our tenderly tended slices
of the village pie.

Perhaps I'll hang a house and a feeder
to lure these songsters
these blues and yellows
browns and reds
into my domesticity.

But really what I want is
that lift at my shoulder blades
that unfolding of wings
that unrehearsed melody
as I take to the air
through the open window.

Ode to Grove Street

Does anyone come knocking
on your door
anymore
(besides the FedEx delivery knock
or the UPS tap and flee
or the USPS carrier
if the package doesn't fit in your mailbox)?

Who visits unannounced
these days
or brings you dates and spinach pies
for no other reason
than that she likes them
and maybe you do, too?

Where else can you attend
an ice cream social
in someone's backyard?

Or hear an electric guitar wailing
to scare up some ghosts
on Halloween night?

Or eat shortbread dipped in chocolate
on Christmas Eve?

What sprites leave eggs
decorated like geishas and ballerinas
on your doorstep
on Easter morning?

Who helps you
look for your lost kitten
or consoles your broken heart
when your puppy runs into the street?

Who borrows your tools
and helps you fix your broken gate?

And where are the neighborhoods
where kids ride their bikes in the road
and build forts
in their front yard?

Where everyone's invited
to pick sweet, red raspberries
in August?

Where the Memorial Day parade
gets shorter every year
and the town's band gets older
and forgets to play their songs
as they roll by on the flatbed truck
but we stand on the corner anyway
waving at the Little League
and the high school marching band
and the fire trucks,
wouldn't miss the chance
to eat Gayle's French toast
and hear how the neighbors
made it through the winter.

And what other wild summer garden
is home to so many hummingbirds?

And where else do your neighbors
bring you squash soup
when you're sick?
Or trundle over
with a wheelbarrow
full of chicken manure and wood shavings,
just the thing for your compost recipe?

Well, I'm not telling . . .
because then the PR people
will brand us as "the way life should be"
and the Chamber of Commerce
will put us on their website
and the tourists will come
to take pictures with their iPhones.

Even though none of us are saints
and none of us are angels,
but we get along just fine.

We give each other some space,
don't try too hard
to be neighborly,
just enough
so we all know
that if someone comes knocking at the door
we don't think twice
because it's no big deal
it's just the way life should be.

The Islands of Summer

On an island in summer
in a forest unmarked
where moss covers bark
where ferns are deep
feathers of green
and sunlight only occasionally
warms your brow . . .

Bones

Bones and bits
of bird flesh
wet feathers
sticking
to a body skeleton
long and leggy.

How unexpected
an encounter:
death and a bird
at the turn
on a path
of berry bushes
of old trees
and wild iris.

I should have
walked on,
left dumb death
on the wet sand path
to stare forever
from a lidless round eye.

Instead I bent
and touched the wing tip
like a child curious
or a priestess
willing a sign.

The island air
was damp,
the great blue
crooked and broken
but perfectly proportioned
still.

Changed forever by a moment,
his body only slowly
catching up.

The Hermit's Cabin

I've walked this trail
around the island
many times before—
skirted the grassy clearing,
followed the piney path,
picked up the scent
of dampened solitude
pausing reverent
in the broken doorway
of the long deserted cabin,
trespassing on
someone's abandoned memories.

But never 'til today
has the hermit's spirit
hummed this song
of half-remembered dreams;
never has the rocky sun
so burned my eyes
or the air been so still.

It must be the August moon
damp and half-round
pulling itself up
into the fog-heavy sky.

It's not that I long for summer
not to pass;
it's the sweetness of the chickweed
in its second bloom,
the soft salty green of orache
on my tongue.

Poet Edna St. Vincent Millay (1892-1950),
who liked to be called Vincent, grew up in
Camden, Maine. She loved the sea and the
islands. I like to think her spirit lingers here or
at least visits regularly.

To Vincent, on an Island off the Coast of Maine

She is there, somewhere on the island,
wandering now at last still and alone
passing through hemlock and
blue black spruce.

Cold, wet fog leads her to the ragged
cliff edge
where once the horizon
lifted its weight,
where now she walks
over wind-scraped land
over spare soil
and pale, hardscrabble lichens.

She defies beauty to return,
promises one more sonnet,
leans into the wind.

She is there, somewhere on the island.
Unable to rest
she searches the seawall for missing stones,
hoping to peer through.
She tests for a rent in the veil
of illusion, knows death
for the strange thing it is.

Where Nothing Approaches Unseen

On Buckle Island
a great blue heron
suddenly
with long stir-fork legs
hanging
from a beating of feathers
leapt
from a treetop
inside a spruce wood
so determined
above
the dry stillness
of fallen tree limbs
and mid-July.

The sun spread
yellow-gray through
the high summer
sea haze.

I walked
the slender
inkling
of a path
over stones
deep in moss.

Why the creature
did not stay still
and smell my sweat
and hear the conversations
in my head
why it did not know
I wouldn't harm it why?

It bunched and vaulted
over the dead trunks and branches
and landed
I suppose
on a shore rock
open to the wind
where nothing approaches unseen.

Stone Wall

Coming across the old stone wall
pocked with lichens
and covered with brambles.

An old fence, too,
with a gate that opens
to nothing used or lived in,
a gate nonetheless.

There's something about
simply coming across a place
where people used to live
and now don't
on a warm spring afternoon.

Where someone's arms and shoulders
lifted slabs and rounds of rock
and nested them to lie
in so intimate conjugation
for safety or solitude,
intrusions or edges,
boundaries more likely, or beauty,
beauty that is mine now,
whether intended
or the stray consequence
of a stranger's plans.

Years of absence
hang in the muted air
of this meadow
gone to seed and grown wild.

The dramas great or minor
of time unspent:
babies growing
while you're not watching,
apples falling
unheeded to the ground,
the letter unread on the table,
the longing to know
what makes this stone wall so familiar

when I know I've never been here
before this warm spring afternoon.

Spider Woman North

Among the cool mossy pines
you string up
your soft sticky gossamers.

Spinner weaver
fiber artist of the forest
when the eyes of the night are wide awake
you swing from bush to branch
setting the lace cloth on the table
inviting dinner to your doorstep.

In the morning
I walk the woodland paths
crashing blindly into your loom.
Snatches of your finery
cling to my clumsy arms
thin smears of silk
stretch across my cheeks.

In the near and far corners
of my house of wood and glass
your children and grandchildren
take up residence.
I sweep them up
put them out
they come back in
patiently dress their looms
and resume their plucky lives.

They weave me into their dreams.
Threads and dances
gather at midnight
to tell stories of
tapestries lighter than air
webs stronger than the wind.

I turn in my sleep
but do not wake.

Hog Island Sonnet, Passamaquoddy Bay
(which becomes three islets at low tide)

This island here that is not three, but one,
Whose neck and waist encircled are by tides,
Whose sash and collar never clean will come
Of mud and muck its coastline streams to hide;

This island is a planet bound so soon
By streams of weeds in random constellation,
Borne now by currents, now by gale or moon:
The fluid green frontier of this sea nation.

I circumnavigate it in my skiff;
I go ashore in search of berries red,
Of roses pink, of shells and sticks adrift,
Of lavender in bunches in its beds.

There is no garden sweeter that I know,
Than one without the scars of plow or hoe.

In the Distance

In the distance
a blue heron
at large in flight
ungainly wing span
neck of necks
enigmatically looped
he lands at the edge
of reeds and mud
king of marshes
royal hunter of fishes
beak like a sword
he sights his prey
lengthens and thrusts
the elegant hose neck
majestic loner
of blue-gray proportions.

Knowing full well
I am watching
he ignores me
on one leg
posed
for more important conquests.

As I approach
he fans his wings
lifts
and forgets me.

For a moment
I am lonelier
than I know,
receding,
my spirit unhooked
like a winded kite.

In the amnesia of insight
I write this
as if
you too
were hearing
the wings beat
the salt air
feeling the feathers
circle your throat
as the blue heron
leaves you
with this same
unspeakable longing.

I suspect these words
are not enough,
slant and unstable as they are,
sodden with ink and overuse,
to thread my sight
through your eyes
to follow his flight
of hollow bones
and wet feathers.

All the same
I walk home
picking up words
like stones from a beach
placing them
in twos and threes
looking for a pattern
that speaks
this language.

Sea Lavender
Limonium carolinianum

Her territory:
the essence of temporary,
the uncertain, beaten, worn
and ever-moving,
ever-changing breath
where sea and moon
exchange their greetings.

She thrives,
indeed can only survive
among shore rocks and marsh grasses,
her roots anchored
in soft and spongy sea mud.

The air she breathes is cold and salty.
Her taut, thin stems,
wrapped in seaweed
and the papery remains of crabs,
branch into spikey statements
of tiny blue-gray flowers,
sprays of pale delicacy
that hint at her tough tenderness.

She's weathered a lot of storms,
has many tales to tell.
But she saves them.
And when all the other flowers
are dead or dormant
and it's winter
and we look for warmth and stories,
there she is,
reminding us
that the tide advances
and the tide recedes,
so send your roots down deep
and hold your head up high.

Each in Its Season

The year turns on its wheel.
The river flows unfrozen.
Life holds us close.

January Snow

This gift of January snow
that stops me
in mid-sentence
blankets my car
says: stay home today

sit by the stove
sip from this white china cup
its coffee warm and woody
the cream and frost
of winter inside and out

make room
for the thoughtful placing
of ferns and fibers
to shape the contours
of this nest of
breath and bone

slow down until
there is just not enough time
for all the important tasks
you planned to accomplish

until setting the table
becomes a ritual
of symmetry

peeling an orange
a sacrament of the senses.

No need, winter says,
to leap from sky to sky,
flying over time zones,
when
it is an adventure
to land on this moment
to choose each word
to sip this cup of coffee
to hear, as if for the first time,
the snow melting on the roof.

Be as a Tree

It's February today
and the Norway maple
is a cold pillar of tree
gaunt and silver-gray
sap frozen
in place
roots anchored
in the cold, cold ground.

Winter chickadees flit and sing
in its wings
scrappy squirrels race
along its corridors
ice coats its shoulders.

No one seems
anxious for the stirring
not yet released.

Just be as a tree
I remind myself.

Spring Never Comes

Spring never comes when you need her.
But here she is:
a promise
of mud and moss
melting ice
this day slightly longer
than the others
a small hard bud
on a branch.

She's out there now—
not the delicate maiden Spring
of fragrant blossom and pale petal—
she comes later.

But first. . .
the warrior stream
raging against
the gray sleep of February.

Then March
thawing the pond
heating the sap
unbuttoning our sins
and paying our debts

so April can remember
and return to us
what was taken away
what we let slip away
what we long for
as we watch for
the pale yellow petals of May.

April in Maine

Sometimes I want nothing
but to stand boot-deep in spring mud,
to poke around the flower beds
in the chill April air,
to listen to
this heaving subterranean
gardener at work
on the seasonal meanings
of seeds and bulbs and roots
and the wordless awakenings
and the perfect beginnings of things.

I cry easily these days,
sleep lightly.

Has life always been this sweet?

Or is it because it is barely spring
and through the cold rain and salt,
in the most improbable
and in some of the desired
places hard green shoots
the tough bulbs of April in Maine
are finding their way back?

I remember, watching them,
the long nights spent waiting,
the despair that comes
from living
where things really die,
where one need not feign surprise
that tender-lipped violets
are resurrected
from the frozen land.

The garden is ragged with
crumpled leaf heaps
and straw mulch pushed aside by
the rubber knights of tulips
the spongy knives of narcissus.

The accumulation of cycles
looks in April like unmeshed gears
and broken bones.
In May it seems to work as if effortlessly,
like things that are never resolved
because they work,
work together,
have never stopped working.

Each in Its Season

It is barely April
and the much maligned dandelion
is among the first arrivals.
She comes hurling herself at our lawns uninvited.
Is that why she is unwelcome?
Radiant little being!
Look at her glowing cheeks
and love her for her steadfast devotion.

Meanwhile, we watch impatiently
for our garden darlings:
the tender tulips of May
the pomp and peonies of June
the irises so independent
lilies lithe and lovely in July's heat.

Following these divas
the umbels of elders flower
like points of sweet cream dappled in a basket
and the heady scent of valerian
soothes our sleep through open windows.

Soon Queen Anne's lace
fringes every field and meadow
and ornamental jewelweed
sways tall and taller, pink and laughing
at the stalwart efforts and dense yellow of goldenrod.

And then the asters of August
appearing right on time,
first as questions,
later as purple answers.

Each in its season.
Each with its reason.
Why here,
why now?
Choosing to live
is all.

Ornamental Jewelweed
Impatiens glandulifera

Oh this jewel of a weed
this bothersome gem
this annual presence
summer resident
nuisance and interloper
growing everywhere
no respect for boundaries
appearing overnight
among the lettuces and nasturtiums
springing up like a jack-in-the-box
stretching her neck
growing fast and tall
laughing and loving
in the heat of summer!

Now that it is the season
when petals wilt and fall
and stems are dry and brittle,
when flowers wild and tame
scatter their seeds,
I look for her pink cheeks
and lanky spine
and am gladdened
when I spy her in the brambles,
by the roadside,
in the hayfield,
along the swale,
a final treat for the wild bees.

Yet I grab hold of her slim waist
and pull her out.
Mind your manners, I tell her,
leave some room for the others.

Autumn Equinox

Today our fall begins.
This is not, however,
reason enough
to slough off so soon
the warm skin of summer
and stand shivering
at the open window
of the winter we all know
is, as we speak,
biding her time
in the hollow pockets
of brazen cold,
furling and unfurling her gusty breath.

For even here,
on the ragged coast of Maine,
is there ever a time or season,
a single day, even,
when nothing stirs?

Hold this day gently, then,
as if a bird
flying south
stunned by the wide and high
world of sky
she was born into
had landed in your hand
and her trip-hammer heart
and brown quivering feathers
were your own whole world
briefly and you scarcely breathed
wanting her to stay
in your palm
cupped like a nest
wanting her to glance up
tilt her bird head listening
as birds do
to the warm drafts of September air
or the scratching of dragonfly legs.

Hold this day gently,
this palm cupped around the memory
of such miracles,
the other hand
waving your visitor farewell
and fair skies.

October Afternoon

The surface of the pond is smooth,
the air peppered with gray and gold
trilling and warbling,
scarlet and black winging and cawing.

A dragonfly, then, yes,
come closer:
your light thin legs of fancy,
your wings, four flights
of drift and sail.
Tired now, this fragile being
alights on my knee,
does asanas with all her legs,
breathes, leaves.

The red and yellow leaves
are brighter than you today,
sun of all my fingers and eyes.

A chipmunk plunges past
colliding with my bare foot,
engaged in October occupations
in the grasses by the shore.

Madame Dragonfly returns,
a red tail thin as a match stick,
six dainty wire legs
and a slick bouffant hairdo.
She languishes in the margin
of my open notebook
like an elegant brooch
for a lady's blouse,
so tired she doesn't stir
when I shift my leg.
Is she resting or dying
as the sun shines its cool blue
October afternoon light?

Another Madame lands.
She looks up at me
with light bulb eyes,
pooches her lips
and slides her six legs
over my calligraphy
and orthography.

An iridescent green bug
sidles up to a black ant.

Strands of my blond and gray hair
sway like tall grasses
among fallen logs.

The surface shifts slightly
as a breeze treads water,
skims light and cool
over the far side of the pond.

Trees like orange bonfires
ribbon their images on the water,
wavy as a mirror of dappled glass.

Thin cloud versions pass
like tourists
having a look.

I wish this October afternoon
could last a bit longer.
There are memories and acorns
to store up for winter.

November

Nothing hurts so much
as November.
Hardly anything left.
A few stalks.

The sun creeps away early.
When it slinks back
it never lingers.
A shadow of its former self,
like the limp tail of a comet
you think you remember.

The rain comes cold.
We slide downhill
until it snows
not even knowing enough
to hold on.

Don't call me by my name today.
I can't return the favor.

I have dropped all my leaves.
Nothing left but trunks
and the bare branches of things.

The turtles know what to do in November,
so do the squirrels and bears
and hyacinth bulbs.

Only the geese are rowdy now,
honking and raucous sky plows
making their way down south.

In the Dark

Sun ball rolling
on your way to heaven
come back
wait for us
don't go alone!

Don't leave us
in the dark
weighing our words

heaving sacks of stones
into the river

troubled without knowing why

uncertain of the time and place

silent
when there is
so much to say.

Winter Solstice

On the longest,
darkest night of the year
a noble deer appears
at the northern edge
of the starless sky,
her antlers branched
like the brown limbs
of brooding oaks.

Through winter's frozen curtain
shines a pale light
and then another
and another growing brighter
as Mother Deer carries aloft
the life of the new sun
like candles on the tree of life.

Watch as she flies
over the sleeping houses
leaving the gift of warmth,
the blessings of light,
the promise of the sun's return.